7/28/06

Elliott Elizabeth,

may you always
be happy as you grow
to know the world.

Tom, Liz, + Annette
Jochum

# Reach for the Sky
## and other little lessons
## for a happier world

Written by
Allison Stoutland

Illustrated by
Cathy Hofher

inch by inch
PUBLICATIONS

# One person can make a difference, and every person should try.

– John Fitzgerald Kennedy

*We wish to acknowledge the following people who have truly made a difference to us: Aunt Nancy and Uncle Ira Gouterman, Karen Elyse, Michael N. Aquino, Esq., Keith Sipe and Linda Lacy, for their advice and support; the teachers and children at Enders Road Elementary School in Manlius, NY, for enthusiastically "testing" our product; our families, for their love and total faith in us; and the myriad of friends who have taken REACH FOR THE SKY under their angel wings...*
*Thank you!*

Text copyright © 1999 by Allison Stoutland
Illustrations copyright © 1999 by Cathy Hofher

Published by
**INCH BY INCH PUBLICATIONS, LLC**

Library of Congress Catalog Card Number: 99-61517
ISBN 0-9670941-0-0

To my kids
who knew me
as Miss Allison;
and to my kids who know me
as Mom...
never, *ever* give up.
— a.j.s.

To Jim,
who taught me
that laughing out loud
is good for the soul;
and to Tara, Shannon and Molly,
who make me smile
from the inside out.
— c.h.

# Bees
## taught me...

that cooperating with each other gets the job done.

# Flowers
## taught me...

that everything needs water to survive.

# Swans
# taught me...

that, sometimes, growing up can be difficult.

# My dog
## taught me...

that there's no one quite as special as your

best friend.

Cats

taught me...

that lying in a sunny spot is a

wonderful feeling.

# Snowflakes taught me...

are exactly the same.

that no two people

Clouds
taught me...

that beauty comes in all shapes and sizes.

The inchworm
taught me...

to never, ever, give up.

Snowmen
taught me...

that sometimes · things you love go away.

# Pigs
## taught me...

that getting · dirty is okay.

# Giraffes
# taught me...

to r-e-a-c-h for the sky!

# Turtles
# taught me...

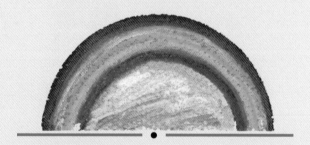

that it is important to protect myself sometimes.

# The owl
# taught me...

to appreciate the moon and the stars.

# Bears
## taught me...

that snuggling up for the night invites sweet dreams.

# inch by inch

PUBLICATIONS

www.inchbyinchbooks.com